C·2

ERIK SATIE
Twenty Short Pieces for Piano

(SPORTS ET DIVERTISSEMENTS)

Illustrations by Charles Martin

Dover Publications, Inc., New York

The publisher is grateful to Leonard Fox, Ltd., Rare Books, 667 Madison Avenue, New York, N.Y. 10021 for making an original copy of this rare portfolio available for direct photographic reproduction.

This Dover edition, first published in 1982, is a republication of the portfolio *Sports et Divertissements*, originally published by Publications Lucien Vogel, Paris, n.d. [ca. 1925] in a limited edition of 225 copies (plus 675 copies with only one illustration). The original table of contents and the half-title pages preceding the pieces of music have been omitted for reasons of space. All the illustrations were originally in color (hand-colored in the pochoir process by Jules Saudé); the present edition reproduces them in black-and-white with only one in color on the front cover. The Publisher's Note, the French-and-English table of contents and the complete translations of the texts have been prepared by Stanley Appelbaum specially for this Dover edition.

International Standard Book Number: 0-486-24365-6

Manufactured in the United States of America
Dover Publications, Inc.
180 Varick Street
New York, N.Y. 10014

Publisher's Note

In the immediate post-Wagnerian era, characterized largely by empty grandiloquence and interminable pieces written for massive performing forces, the French composer Erik Satie (1866–1925) emerged as a master of musical understatement and a champion of the expressive miniature. His unique blending of austere quietism and acid wit, his innovative harmonies and freedom of form made a strong impression on Debussy and Ravel, and then on such younger composers as Poulenc and the other members of Les Six. The general public began to recognize Satie's great merit a few decades ago, and now his place as a highly influential minor master is secure.

Among the half-dozen works by Satie which the English musicologist Rollo H. Myers has stated "are outstanding and cannot by ignored by any student of contemporary music" is the set of twenty piano miniatures called *Sports et Divertissements* (Sports and Pastimes). "These little masterpieces of wit and ironic observation," Myers says of the *Sports et Divertissements*, "reveal his genius perhaps more convincingly than any other of his works, with the exception of [the cantata] *Socrate*." Patrick Gowers, writing in *The New Grove Dictionary of Music and Musicians* (1980), considers this set as the "apotheosis" of Satie's mature, lean piano style. The work has also been acclaimed by such fellow composers as Darius Milhaud and such great performers as Alfred Cortot.

The present volume reproduces this important music in the exact form in which it originally appeared: in the composer's own superb calligraphy within the rare, luxurious portfolio published by Lucien Vogel (see the copyright statement on the opposite page for bibliographic details). Toward the beginning of 1914 Vogel, publisher of such chic art magazines as the *Gazette du Bon Ton*, asked Igor Stravinsky to compose some short piano pieces to accompany drawings by Charles Martin, one of the most fashionable illustrators of the time. Stravinsky asked for a fee that was considered excessive, whereas the unworldly and dedicated Satie, when he was approached, found a much smaller fee still too high!—but agreed to do the job. The earliest of the pieces, "Fishing," is dated March 14, 1914, and the latest is "Golf," dated May 20, 1914. Publication was no doubt delayed by the outbreak of the First World War, and was not accomplished until well into the Twenties.

In the new complete English translations of Satie's witty accompanying comments, which appear opposite the music pages, the italic type corresponds to the tempo and dynamic indications.

Contents

OPPOSITE: Original title page.

Sports & Divertissements.

MUSIQUE DE
RIK. SATIE

DESSINS DE
CH. MARTIN

PUBLICATIONS LUCIEN VOGEL, 11 RUE SAINT-FLORENTIN, PARIS

Préface

Cette publication est constituée de deux éléments artistiques : dessin, musique.

La partie dessin est figurée par des traits — des traits d'esprit ; la partie musicale est représentée par des points — des points noirs. Ces deux parties réunies — en un seul volume — forment un tout : un album. Je conseille de feuilleter, ce livre, d'un doigt aimable & souriant ; car c'est ici une œuvre de fantaisie. Que l'on n'y voie pas autre chose.

Pour les "Recoquillés" & les "Abètis", j'ai écrit un choral grave & convenable.

Ce choral est une sorte de préambule amer, une manière d'introduction austère & infrivole.

J'y ai mis tout ce que je connais sur l'Ennui.

Je dédie ce choral à ceux qui ne m'aiment pas.

Je me retire.

Erik SATIE

Choral inappétissant

Preface

This publication consists of two artistic elements: drawing, music. The drawing part is composed of lines — witty lines [a pun: *trait d'esprit* = "witty remark"]; the musical part is represented by dots — black dots [also means "blackheads"]. These two parts combined — in a single volume — form a whole: an album. My advice is to leaf through this book with a kindly & smiling finger, for it is a work of imagination. Don't look for anything else in it.

For the Shriveled Up and the Stupefied I have written a serious & proper chorale. This chorale is a sort of bitter preamble, a kind of austere & un-frivolous introduction. I have put into it all I know about Boredom. I dedicate this chorale to those who don't like me. I withdraw.

ERIK SATIE

[Translation of Satie's comments that appear with the music:]

UNAPPETIZING CHORALE. *Seriously. Surly & peevish. Hypocritically. More slowly.* MAY 15, 1914 (in the morning, before eating).

La Balançoire

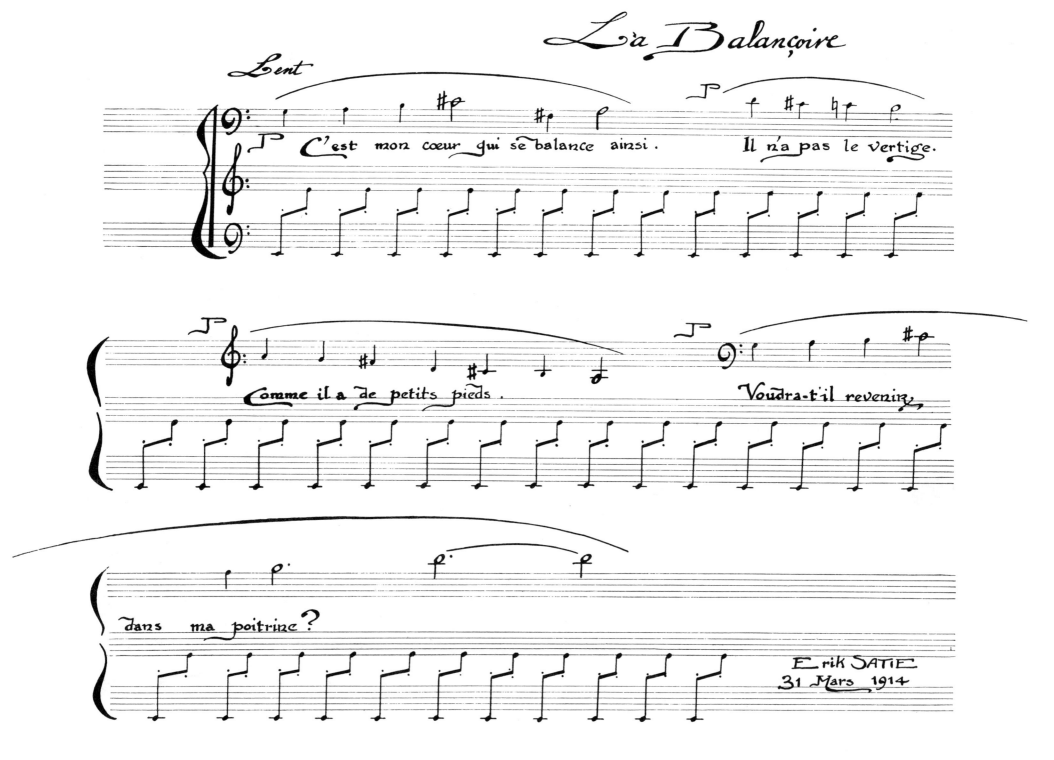

C'est mon coeur qui se balance ainsi. Il n'a pas le vertige.

Comme il a de petits pieds. Voudra-t'il revenir

dans ma poitrine?

Erik SATIE
31 Mars 1914

THE SWING. *Slowly.* It's my heart that is swinging like this. It isn't dizzy. What little feet it has. Will it be willing to return to my breast? MARCH 31, 1914.

La Chasse

Entendez-vous le lapin qui chante?

Quelle voix!

Le hibou allaite ses enfants.

Le rossignol est dans son terrier.

Le marcassin va se marier.

Moi, j'abats des noix à coups de fusil.

7 Avril 1914

Erik SATIE

HUNTING. *Fast.* Do you hear the rabbit singing? What a voice! The nightingale is in its burrow. The owl is nursing its children. The young wild boar is going to get married. As for me, I am knocking down nuts with rifle shots. APRIL 7, 1914.

La Comédie italienne

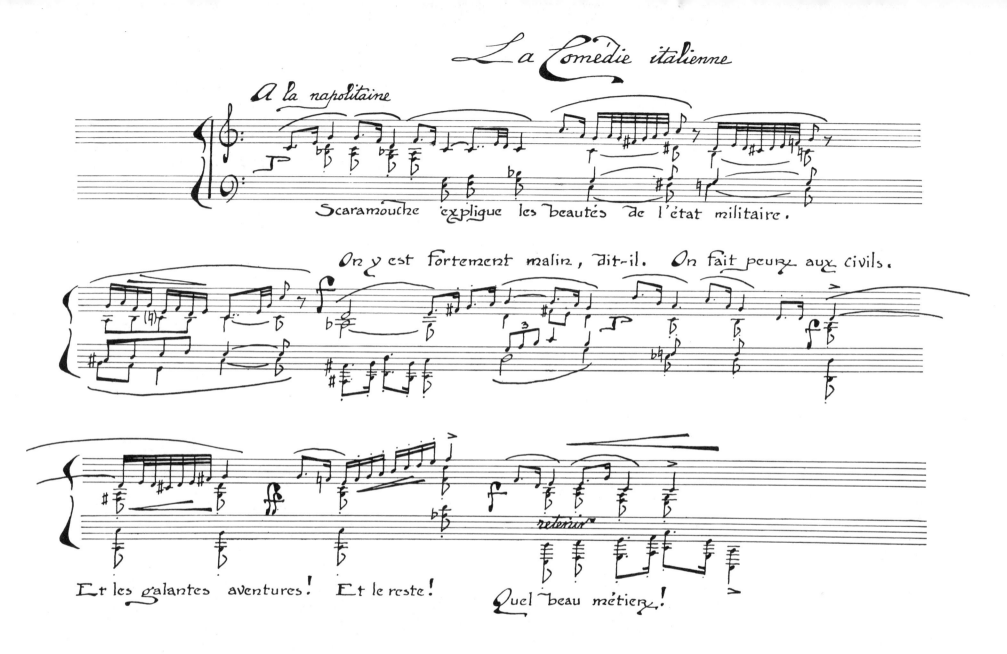

A la napolitaine

Scaramouche explique les beautés de l'état militaire.

On y est fortement malin, dit-il. On fait peur aux civils.

Et les galantes aventures! Et le reste!

Quel beau métier!

Erik SATIE
29 Avril 1914

THE ITALIAN COMEDY. *In Neapolitan style.* Scaramouche is explaining the beauties of military life. "Soldiers are terrifically sharp," he says. "They frighten the civilians. And their amorous escapades! And all the rest! What a wonderful profession!" APRIL 29, 1914.

Le Réveil de la Mariée

Vif, sans trop

Arrivée du cortège.

Appels.

Levez-vous!

Guitares faites avec de vieux chapeaux.

Un chien danse avec sa fiancée.

sec

Erik SATIE

16 Mai 1914

THE AWAKENING OF THE BRIDE. *Fast, but not too*. Arrival of the cortege.
Shouts. Get up! Guitars made of old hats. A dog is dancing with his fiancée.
Dryly. MAY 16, 1914.

15

Colin-Maillard

Petitement

Cherchez, Mademoiselle. Celui qui vous aime est à deux pas.

Comme il est pâle : ses lèvres tremblent.

Vous riez ? Mais vous passez sans

Il tient son cœur à deux mains.

le deviner.

Erik SATIE

27 Avril 1914

Blindman's Buff. *Pettily.* Keep looking, Miss. The man who loves you is right near you. How pale he is: his lips are trembling. You laugh? He is holding his heart with both hands. But you pass by without suspecting his presence. April 27, 1914.

La Pêche

FISHING. *Calmly.* Murmurs of the water in a stream bed. Arrival of a fish, of another, of two others. "What's up?" "It's a fisherman, a poor fisherman." "Thanks." Everyone goes back home, even the fisherman. Murmurs of the water in a stream bed. MARCH 14, 1914.

Le Yachting

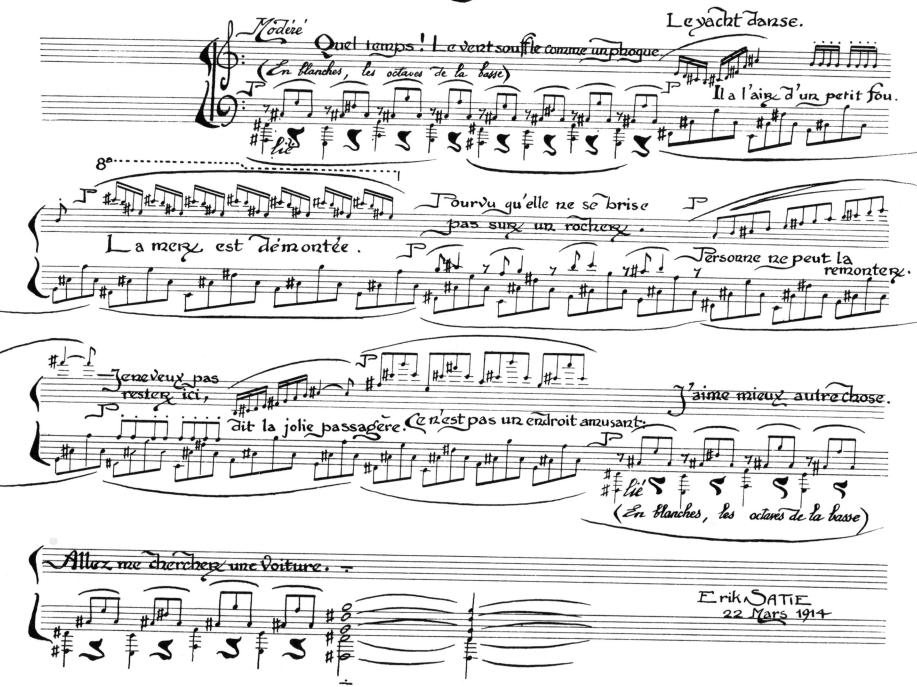

YACHTING. *Moderately. (In half-notes, the octaves of the bass.) Legato.* What weather! The wind is blowing like a sea lion. The yacht is dancing. It acts like a giddy little thing. The sea is raging. I hope it doesn't break on a rock. No one can calm it down [pun on *démontée* and *remonter*]. "I don't want to stay here," says the pretty lady passenger. "It's not an entertaining place. I prefer doing something else. Go get me a car." *Legato. (In half-notes, the octaves of the bass.)* MARCH 22, 1914.

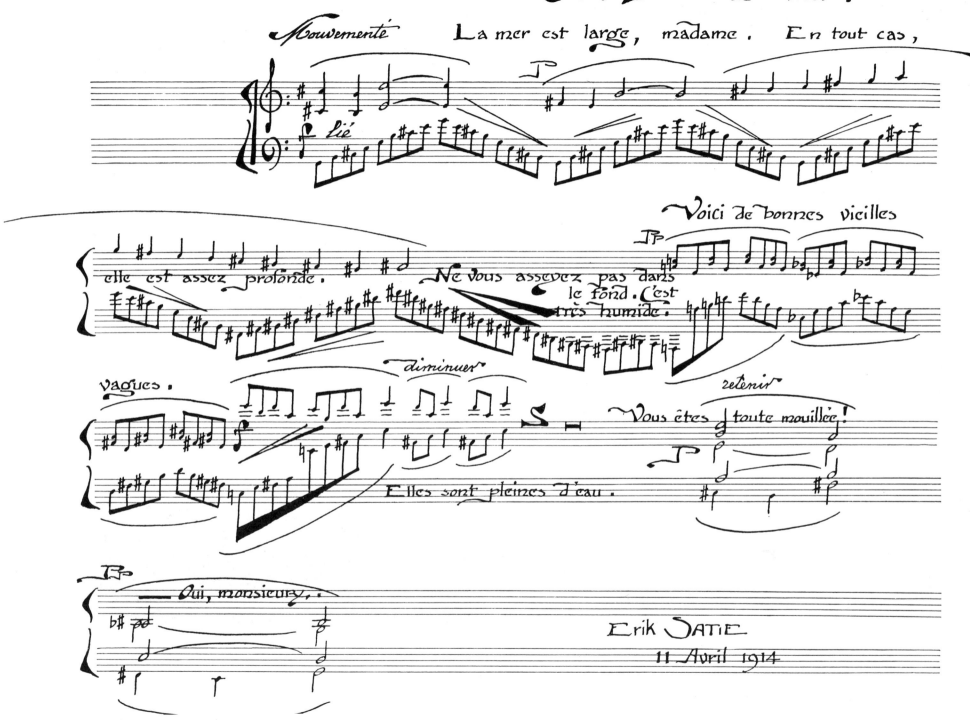

OCEAN BATHING. *Agitatedly.* "The ocean is wide, Madame. Anyway, it's quite deep. Don't sit down at the bottom. It's very damp. Here are some good old waves. *Diminuendo.* They are full of water. *Holding back.* You are all wet!" "Yes, sir." APRIL 11, 1914.

23

Le Carnaval

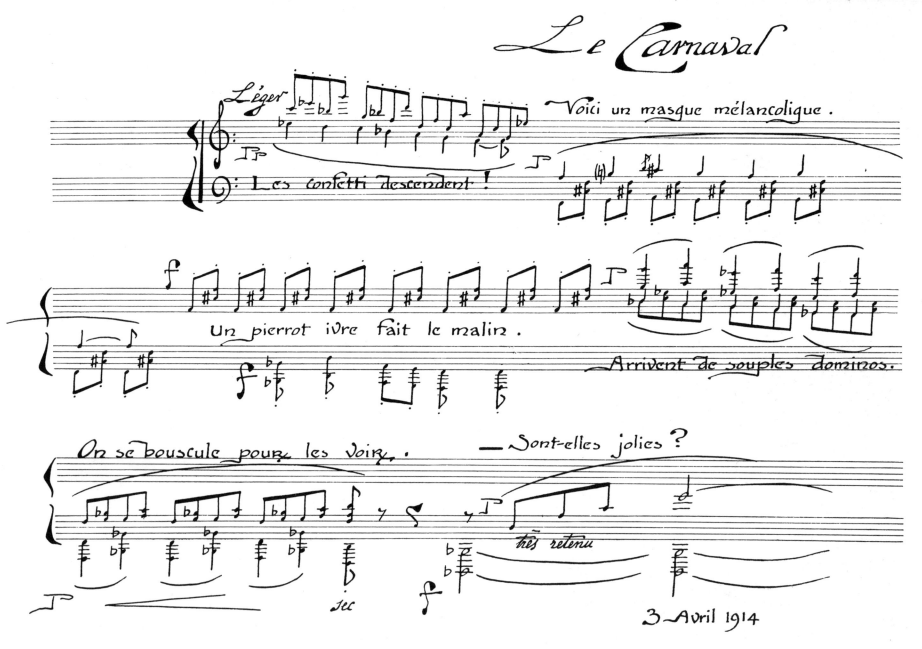

Voici un masque mélancolique.

Les confetti descendent!

Un pierrot ivre fait le malin.

Arrivent de souples dominos.

On se bouscule pour les voir.

— Sont-elles jolies?

très retenu

3 Avril 1914

Erik SATIE

CARNIVAL. *Lightly.* The confetti comes down! Here is a melancholy masker.
An intoxicated Pierrot acts smart. Supple dominos arrive. People jostle one
another to see them. *Dryly.* "Are they pretty?" *Holding back considerably.*
APRIL 3, 1914.

Le Golf

GOLF. *Excitedly.* The colonel is dressed in Scotch tweed of a violent green. He will be victorious. His caddie follows him, carrying the bags. The clouds are surprised. The holes are shaking with fright: "The colonel is here!" Now he makes a fine swing: his club bursts into pieces! MAY 20, 1914.

La Pieuvre

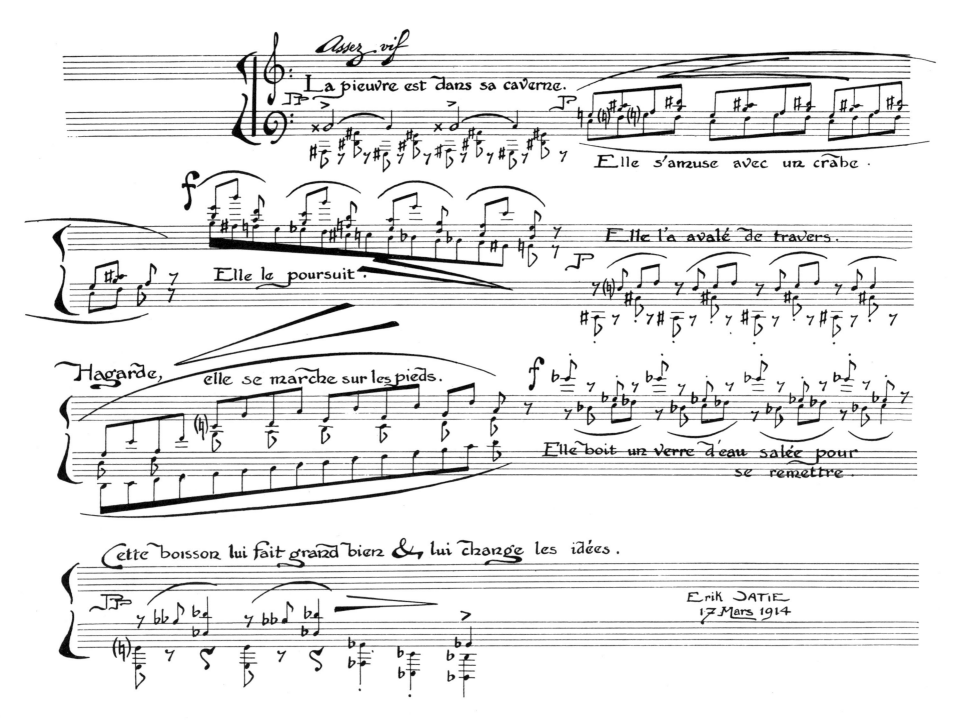

Assez vif

La pieuvre est dans sa caverne.

Elle s'amuse avec un crabe.

Elle l'a avalé de travers.

Elle le poursuit.

Hagarde, elle se marche sur les pieds.

Elle boit un verre d'eau salée pour se remettre.

Cette boisson lui fait grand bien & lui change les idées.

Erik SATIE
17 Mars 1914

28

THE OCTOPUS. *Quite fast.* The octopus is in its cave. It is having fun with a crab. It runs after it. It swallows it, but the crab goes down the wrong way. Its face drawn, the octopus steps on its own feet. It drinks a glass of salt water to recover. That drink does it a lot of good and puts it in a wonderful mood. MARCH 17, 1914.

RACING. *Somewhat fast.* The weighing in. *The crowd.* Buying the program. Twenty & twenty. At the post. Off and running. The horses that swerve and shy. *Diminuendo.* The losing horses (pointed noses & drooping ears). MARCH 26, 1914.

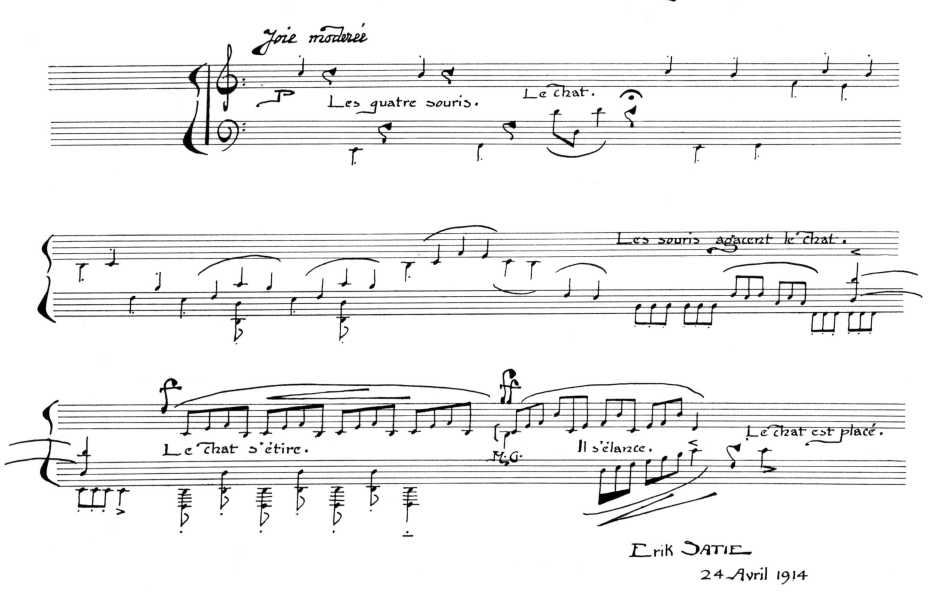

PUSS IN THE CORNER. *Moderated joy.* The four mice. The cat. The mice tease the cat. The cat stretches. *L.H. (left hand).* It darts out. The cat has found a corner. APRIL 24, 1914.

Le Pique-nique

Dansant

Ils ont tous apporté

Vous avez une belle robe blanche.

du veau très froid.

— Mais non : c'est un orage.

— Tiens! un aéroplane.

Erik SATIE
19 Avril 1914

THE PICNIC. *With a dancing movement.* They have all brought very cold veal.
"You have a beautiful white dress." "Look, an airplane!" "Oh, no, it's a storm."
APRIL 19, 1914.

35

SHOOT-THE-CHUTES. *Gracefully.* If you have a strong stomach, you won't be too sick. *Getting louder and holding back.* You will feel as if you were falling off a scaffolding. You'll see how peculiar it is. *Dragging.* Watch out! *Rapidly.* Don't turn all colors. *In tempo.* "I feel awful." *Slowing down.* That proves you needed to have some fun. APRIL 14, 1914.

Le Tango perpétuel

Modéré & très ennuyé

Le tango est la danse du Diable. C'est celle qu'il préfère.

Il la danse pour se refroidir.

Sa femme, ses filles & ses domestiques se refroidissent ainsi.

Erik SATIE
5 Mai 1914

The (Perpetual) Tango. *Moderately and with great boredom.* The tango is the dance of the Devil. It's his favorite. He dances it to cool off. His wife, his daughters & his servants get cool [or: catch a cold] that way. May 5, 1914.

Le Traîneau

Courez

Quel froid !

— Mesdames, le nez dans les fourrures.

Le traîneau file.

Le paysage a très froid & ne sait où se mettre.

Erik Satie
2 Mai 1914

THE SLED. *Running.* How cold it is! *Slowing down. Resuming.* Ladies, keep your noses inside your furs. The sled speeds along. The landscape feels very cold and doesn't know what to do with itself. MAY 2, 1914.

Le Flirt

Agité

lié

— Comment allez-vous?

Ils se disent de jolies choses, des choses modernes.

Ne suis-je pas aimable?

8a

— Laissez-moi?

Vous avez de gros yeux.

Il soupire.

Je voudrais être dans la lune.

Il hoche la tête.

Erik SATIE
29 Mars 1914

42

FLIRTING. *Agitatedly.* They say nice things to each other, modern things. "How are you? I'm likable, right?" "Let me alone. You have big eyes. I'd like to be in the moon." He sighs. He shakes his head. MARCH 29, 1914.

FIREWORKS. *Rapidly.* How dark it is! Oh, a Bengal light! A rocket! A blue, blue
rocket! Everyone admires the show. An old man goes crazy. The last round of
fireworks! APRIL 6, 1914.

45

Le Tennis

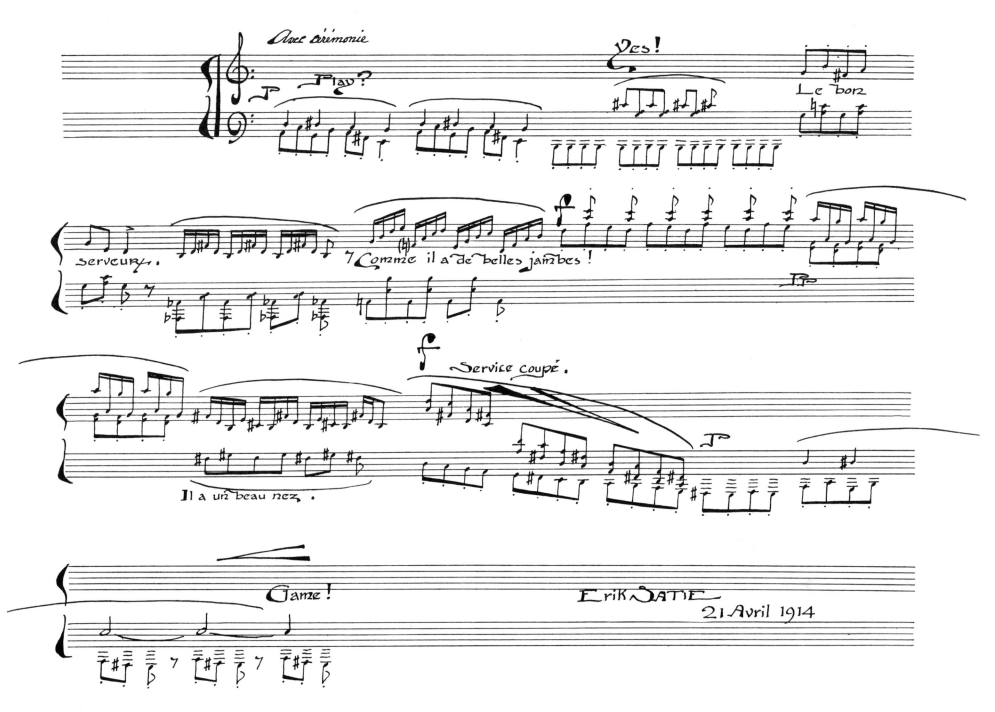

Tennis. *Ceremoniously.* Play? Yes! He has a good serve. What good-looking legs he has! He has a fine nose. A slice serve. Game! April 21, 1914.